and when

the light

comes it will

be so

fantastic

and when the light comes it will be so fantastic

poems

Kristin Berget

TRANSLATED FROM THE NORWEGIAN
BY KATHLEEN MARIS PALTRINERI

CURBSTONE BOOKS / NORTHWESTERN UNIVERSITY PRESS
EVANSTON, ILLINOIS

Curbstone Books

Northwestern University Press

www.nupress.northwestern.edu

Published 2025 by Curbstone Books / Northwestern University Press.

Originally published in Norwegian in 2017 under the title *Og når det blir lyst blir det helt fantastisk*.

This translation has been published with the financial support of NORLA.

Printed in the United States of America

10 9 8 7 6 5 4 3 2 1

LIBRARY OF CONGRESS CATALOGING-IN-PUBLICATION DATA

Names: Berget, Kristin, 1975– author. | Paltrineri, Kathleen Maris, translator.

Title: And when the light comes it will be so fantastic : poems / Kristin Berget, translated from the Norwegian by Kathleen Maris Paltrineri.

Other titles: Og når det blir lyst blir det helt fantastisk. English

Description: Evanston, Illinois : Curbstone Books/Northwestern University Press, 2025

Identifiers: LCCN 2024059253 | ISBN 9780810148468 (paperback) | ISBN 9780810148475 (ebook)

Subjects: LCGFT: Poetry.

Classification: LCC PT8952.12.E745 O413 2025 | DDC 839.821/8—dc23/eng/20241213

LC record available at https://lccn.loc.gov/2024059253

it is after all here
where one
is

—Anna Hallberg, *på era platser* (on your marks), 2004

CONTENTS

This landscape snares us   with its long stalks   A brittle soil fractures in July
We have chosen to scrape our fingers against this earth's crust   get bacteria under our nails
Here we hold tight   Bodies grow give way to new bodies
a system wrought over millions of years   Don't take it personally
that it's crackling   that it's working   It is evolution who speaks
A voice that claims monstrosities

A heart shifts bodies
from animal to human
Tears simulate both
sea and grief
breath a wind
drawing the sea
in and out
from the shore

We are humans here   birth new humans   inhaling sea air or exhaust
Is it the sea rushing inside us   is it the road network navigating through us
is it heat pumping around   magma below   sun above   We can only exist here
This temperate zone

Outside wildgame fences the houses flash past   a shuttered school   maybe a
converted church   Here the secular transgression progresses   the tools glitter
under florescent lights   before a power outage darkens the village
and we light up from the inside

The brain seeks refuge in unused areas
longs for new boundaries
The brain is not autonomous
it is yours and mine to share
cast in the same form
The fire burns in the eyes

We ask for coalheat for the heart

Soon it is over
a body is pushed out of mine
Soon that body is over
soon it is we who sleep
soon it is we who promise
we will lose everything

As we run along a fresh plowed field   we move across vast plains   toward walls
toward the body's lathwork materials   We run along the plow furrow   the ditch where the sun
is mirrored   At the edge of the field
sometimes we were more lonesome in each other's houses

We must gather
all knowledge
that exists about us

We twist
Are torn away

We must recall
who we were

We stand at a fresh plowed field   The clay layer facing air   Soon the furrow is broken by frost

God storms through our minds while she in a darkness
which cannot be determined whether it's outside or inside deadly or only night
or whether the night is the sounds the foliage evergreen needles minerals saying
All signs exist to be deciphered

Even if we have no soul   is there something that draws us in   We have run along
a fresh plowed field   seen the humus layer broken open   energies set free
The exhausted phosphorus   starving clay layer   Somewhere the children sleep
a holy trinity   or two triangles fused into a Star of David
It draws us in

Winter must come with atonement
Branches break   shaded areas turn light   An icy blue air drives us
each in our own direction   We must ready ourselves to comb the terrain tonight   circle in and
map   Frostsmoke floats from our mouths   we must learn to interpret smoke signals
And then a crash over the ice-encrusted moss bed   A stag comes into view
Now animals and humans must walk together

Mythically we take our place before one another   seeking to decipher the bark's depressions
animal wisdom   ancestral whispers   If we are undying
what's so wrong with killing

Then we dig a grave   in the shadow of the family tree   Fill it with bones and feathers
so the forest can swallow the story   We saw branches off the tree   watch darkness fall
through the treetops   Smoke rises from the chimney where we keep house
When later we will sleep   we sing for one another   with thin voices

A fossil song from the plow furrow
or from under the plow furrow
from what the plow furrow unleashes

A fossil saga pulls at the collarbone
or the twenty-six bones that make up the skull

the little animal's imprint in the stone
an insect
and the worm's dark paths

Or are we sleepwalking

I did not dream her
There was no gust in the wind
asking for her

No
There was no body
opening

There wasn't a word in the mouth
that said the dog
that said her

There wasn't a new moon desiring
War is a word that leaves us in ruin for fifty to one hundred years
We must whisper but we shout

Who were we before we had this
the word
I long for you

The desert and the god who wandered in it
Forty days isn't long
There is darkness in the world when the world is dark

I can't go on without explaining that this is by the sea The view then is
of the sea I can add: There's a lighthouse here I want to sleep in the lighthouse but don't
My breasts are leaking the white fluid pours out over a thick wooden tabletop
You might come and demand kinship saying you recognize the wool sweater
It's pitiful to have children you say You won't acknowledge my overabundance
It is the fields then that are the view

Fog pulls
in from the sea
all that can sink
sinks
Is it the lack of air between stones
that makes mammals flee
Reptiles lean against granite
storing the earth's body heat
Time is neither marker
nor passage
The view disappears
into a white dark

I must build a fire   damp is pulling through the walls   Grain is cut down
to ankle height   the gold flecked fields are spreading in the view out there
I set bread dough by the open window   Nothing must be hastened now
the sea can swell at any point

Night will come
again soon
How is darkness
for those who are
where it is always dark
The insignificance of
the earth's orbiting around the sun
seasons that vary
cold-bloodedness that holds
life in place

We must share this

be here in the warmth sheltered from the whimsical sea   it will storm again
The breasts are full of milk that rushes
The mouths: identically sugarstinking
The sea will roll in over the beach   salt dries the lips   seaweed is unwound
from the hair

Now it rushes in

The forests are filling
The tidewater must promise
to take the heather
back with it

The lighthouse lantern flickers asleep   we wake in fits and starts before floating a day and night between
sleeping and waking   Here the mountain air is sharp   the ptarmigans startle   wake us at last
Now the sea rises   draws in over the pebbles   leaving behind shells and gravel
Everything that falls out of boats and ships   can be washed into new forms
collecting at the forest edge for us to gather tomorrow
if the sea draws back

They had taken her from us to weigh and measure her   still bleeding I lay
with my legs high   It was Saturday morning   the light was dim   We must explain to her
about the light   about the dreams made visible on the surface of skin   about the sea
that rises with the tide   about the branches that grow   about the forest that lures

The forest lures

Do not be fooled   this is not a folktale   This is we move steadily
toward darkness   under the wild sweet peas blossoming in the pasture   A sunflower
has been dispersed by means of a bird   And clover   we need the nitrogen
we say   Dropping a bone   just a knee down in the plow furrow

I do not name earth
I do not name god
I do not name I
I do not name oil
or ointment
or the polluted sea
Laying the brow against the cobblestone
opening the palms up to the air
filling the lungs with dust and fluid
expecting one more heat
that rages through the body

The child I name
flame and ash

Nights without sleep   probably I will die tonight   Is this a normal night
God storms through our minds   the forest machines working   the trawlers scraping
the coral reef

All must be forgiven for a moment
There must be some grace
whispering close behind

Lowering us slowly down
binding the nitrogen
extracting the phosphorus
giving back what is not ours
The people of long ago are not remembered,
nor will there be any remembrance
of people yet to come
by those who come after them.
Ecclesiastes 1:11

Now we look at the sea
simultaneously

saying earth
Whispering

agreements
hopes

The water the wine the child
we send them back

This is our last memory: Magma heats the earth's core from the inside
Granite also gives off body heat   A joint loosens and the animal collapses
No one will remember it   no one has seen it
witnesses no longer exist

This is our first memory: The church   seen from across the valley   Snowed over
lit by floodlights
Inside a sacrament is underway   Full vessels are filled   Forgiveness is handed out   We lie

We stand in this dark forest   That is alongside the black ocean
The waves are breaking   The bark is breaking   Voices breaking   The conversations we have each on our own

Evening comes with a new moon   still too weak to light us up   We look
out across the sea   dark as fresh plowed earth   No sound was heard when they held the cold
stethoscope against her chest   The lungs were full of fluid   that wrapped up
the sound of the heart

We should hear the sea lapping
We should glow from the inside

I would like to say it is simple
to love something frail

The dark contour
innermost in the human masses

we suddenly see
is an animal heart

Now we crawl down
from our viewpoint of the world

is it right to step on this exact soil
let the ash cool underfoot

will the birds keep flying two by two and
be an omen of dismal days of dismal nights

will we whisper prayers over the dry sand
not knowing if anyone will answer

is it right to demand an answer from the soil
do minerals build the body heal(s) the wounds

will we bow to this assertion
will we bow to this truth

will we bow to this policy
will we bow to this god

if the night trickles into our blood
the iron darkens and hardens

will we then let this happen
will we then let this happen

will we give thanks for the grace all grace all food
is it right to seek advice is it right to be bewildered

is it right to think are we sleepwalking again
shouldn't we be awake when we're searching

is it right that our love paints the soil red

The real heart pumps in the ribcage
We swaddle sleep and death in the same duvet

Unreality's boundaries are once again displaced

The single rib
cannot create coherence

The hearts can only wail at the wall
torn loose like a family

Our darkening features
the blood left on the duvet

The specific smell of sleep
our sleeping fading eyes

How the spine breaks piece by piece
with each word spoken

and when the light comes it will be so fantastic

That we still exist   over white pages   where we spell our names
repeating the commandments
Night is emptied of angels and signs   The signs exist   only for their decipherers
We are not seeresses but religious   Our endless attempts at naming

If only we had been silent long enough   Through the wall
this labyrinthian city's noise drifts away   We don't know what kind of consequence there will be
as a result   when the face comes into view   Again the ash
We can never promise each other anything within language or the wall
Of course we should have chosen other words
We cannot ask for understanding

Go to the grave
alternatively to the grave
or just the grave
At the edge lies the desert blank
Her little hand
the raw flesh

It must be emptied
to be filled
to fall to the ground
foliage apples grenades dust
Your hand in mine
The pendulum swinging
We invented the word
sleep and said
This is an action
lie down here and rest
perhaps an angel
guards your sleep
your dust

In our hands we carry oil salt bread   fall into each other's arms
This ritual act   will loosen   the hate we bear
We will say   the children sleep   everyone sleeps   This is a ceremony   every word is a prayer
the prayer is a practice   the practice is endurance

Now that we have become lost
come down from the heights
toward the wall
Now that our languages
blow about
It is morning and morning
words are earth
Now that we've come loose
leaping in every direction
Now that we are entirely literal

Night seeps into the blood
the iron dark and hard

Lets it happen

TRANSLATOR'S NOTE

Translating Norwegian poet Kristin Berget's *and when the light comes it will be so fantastic* during a natural disaster and a global pandemic was an uncanny experience. The destabilization on the page was often mirrored by the precarity of life before me. With steady wind speeds of one hundred and forty miles per hour, the 2020 derecho had irrevocably altered the landscape of my hometown of Cedar Rapids, Iowa. City officials estimate that 669,000 mature trees, or roughly seventy percent of its canopy, were lost; and in nearby Solon, where I was living, I watched the largest branch of a black walnut tree split from the trunk after a strong gust during the storm. The derecho claimed four human lives, left over half of a million people across the state without electricity, and caused an emergency shutdown of a nuclear power plant. Amidst all of this, the volatile world of Berget's book felt close at hand.

This collection, the first of Berget's numerous literary works to be translated into English, contains vast time scales, anxieties about the future, and images of rising seas, cultivated fields, and animated forests. The reader has the feeling that she's entered the world of the poems after a cataclysmic, yet ambiguous, loss. There is a birth story, one that is shrouded in precarity. Bodies are written upon. The human body is paralleled with the furrow in the field; personal loss and collective loss are enmeshed. As such, Berget's poetry invites pressing questions: How do we mourn both human and ecological losses? Is there a boundary between the two? And how do these losses shape human consciousness?

The mutability of the poems' environments is forever present, forever imminent, and is revealed both in imagery and in the friction of rushed and interrupted syntax, like the jostling of verbs against one another. In what can be read as an ecopoetic method of composition, Berget's use across the book of repetend, such as *a fresh plowed field*, and anaphoric phrases—*is it right*, *will*, *if*, and so on—become a kind of recycling of language. The following poem and its phrase *can be washed into new forms* served as a lodestar for my reading of the book's thematic concerns and compositional modes.

The lighthouse lantern flickers asleep   we wake in fits and starts before floating a day and night between
sleeping and waking   Here the mountain air is sharp   the ptarmigans startle   wake us at last
Now the sea rises   draws in over the pebbles   leaving behind shells and gravel
Everything that falls out of boats and ships   can be washed into new forms
collecting at the forest edge for us to gather tomorrow
if the sea draws back

As exemplified here, Berget's poems point to the continual decomposing, processing, and repurposing of all material life, and the recycled language in her poetry linguistically enacts the experience of living within the detritus of the climate crisis.

As I recognized Berget's ecologies of language, my own ecotranslation practices began to take shape. Where a verb (*driver*) was repeated in the Norwegian to link the force of breast milk with the force of the sea, I also repeated the same verb (*rushes*) in the English to carry forward the connection, taking care not to turn to that verb to describe other actions. Where the poems rely on the passive voice to suggest the bodies are being acted upon from the outside, I also used passive voice. Where the poems insisted on the use of the word *plow furrow* (*plogfure*) when the word *furrow* (*fure*) alone is also available in the Norwegian, I insisted on the use of *plow furrow*, identifying *plow furrow* as a kind of anti-pastoral gesture, or critique of industrial agriculture and the cultures that valorize it. As I translated, it was important to me to recreate the intimacy with the material world as well as the distance, disconnection, and destruction.

Berget writes in Bokmål, one of the two Norwegian-language scripts, both of which contain three additional vowels—æ, ø, å—in comparison to the English alphabet. As a translator, my aim was to listen carefully to the alliteration and assonance of Berget's poetry, and to hear the spatially extended caesuras as much as I saw them. Drawn to Berget's rhythms, I endeavored to rewrite her poems into a lyrical English, noting the sounds and how they inform meaning and feeling. Translation, like poetry, is an embodied art. I translated by hand, reading aloud the furrow-like lines, first by phrase, and then attended to each syllable. The pleasure of the sounds buzzed in my throat as I wrote.

Berget's poetry suggests that just as we have invented language, we have also invented a lack of awareness. Awareness exists, but we often disappoint it. Even so, language also emerges in these poems as a ritual cycle, not as redemption, but as an attempt toward wholeness by reaching for one another. She writes,

In our hands we carry oil salt bread   fall into each other's arms
This ritual act   will loosen   the hate we bear
We will say   the children sleep   everyone sleeps   This is a ceremony   every word is a prayer
the prayer is a practice   the practice is endurance

Translating these poems has become my own ritual act in the face of a natural disaster and a pandemic. Translation has become one of my own ways to attend to life.

After the initial shock of the derecho, our neighborhood began hauling tree branches out of the road—a one way circle—carefully avoiding downed powerlines so that people could safely get to the supplies they needed. Months later, once lives were mourned and homes were patched up, people began memorializing lost trees and planting new ones. The uprooted trees that lined the streets, the downed branches, the jagged limbs of those still standing reminded me of Berget's invitation to reimagine our human relationship to nature and to each other.

KATHLEEN MARIS PALTRINERI

Alongside the black walnut tree

ACKNOWLEDGMENTS

Many thanks go to my professors and peers at the University of Iowa's MFA in Literary Translation without whom much of my thinking and being as a translator and writer would not be realized. Thank you also to Aron Aji, Kristin Berget, Jenna Coughlin, Jennifer Croft, Eirill Alvide Falck, Louisa Hall, Annie Janusch, Alana Marie Levinson-LaBrosse, Marc Paltrineri, David M. Smith, Jan Steyn, and Elizabeth Willis for your insights into the poems and my translations. I'm grateful for research support from an Iowa Stanley Graduate International Research Award and from a Fulbright Fellowship to Norway. Thank you to my advisors and friends at the University of Tromsø and the University of Oslo, especially Henning Howlid Wærp, Lisbeth Pettersen Wærp, and Sissel Furuseth. Much gratitude to the University of Oslo Department of Linguistics and Scandinavian Studies and the Oslo School of Environmental Humanities for inviting me to speak about my translations. Tusen hjertelig takk to my Norwegian language teachers and tutors throughout the years for reconnecting me to the language of my family. Thank you to my mentors, students, and friends in the University of Iowa English Department. The revision of these poems was made possible while I was a CLAS Postgraduate Visiting Writer of Literary Translation.

Thank you to my editors, Marisa Siegel and Anne Gendler, for your enthusiasm and trust. Tremendous thanks to Aron Aji and Gabriel Gudding for offering their generous words. I'm grateful to the editors of the following literary magazines and sites where versions of these translations first appeared: *Brink*, *Circumference Magazine*, *Guernica*, and *Poetry in Action*, The Action Books Blog. Thank you to the lovely folks at Cappelen Damm, and NORLA, Norwegian Literature Abroad, for your advocacy of Norwegian poetry in translation. This translation has been published with the financial support of NORLA.

Marc Paltrineri, I am lucky to walk this path together with you. Thank you. Loving gratitude to my family and friends for your care and encouragement. Kristin Berget, thank you for sharing your poetry with me. I am indebted to your kindness and your light.